THE ALCHEMIST LEADER

HOW TO DESIGN MEETINGS THAT BUILD TRUST, COOPERATION AND ENGAGES PEOPLE TO WANT TO CREATE EXCELLENCE

TOUCH STONE PUBLISHERS

BE MORE THAN YOU HAVE BEEN

WITH GLENN E DANIELS II

LEADERSHIP SKILLS AND TECHNIQUES

A Story of Excellence

THE ALCHEMIST LEADER

HOW TO DESIGN MEETINGS THAT BUILD TRUST, COOPERATION, AND ENGAGES PEOPLE TO WANT TO CREATE EXCELLENCE

BY GLENN E DANIELS II

Copyrights © Reserved

This book and its content is copyright of [Touch Stone Publishers] - © [Touch Stone Publishers] [2020]. All rights reserved.

Any redistribution or reproduction of part or all of the contents in any form is prohibited other than the following:

- you may print or download to a local hard disk extracts for your personal and non-commercial use only
- you may copy the content to individual third parties for their personal use, but only if you acknowledge the book as the source of the material

You may not, except with our express written permission, distribute or commercially exploit the content. Nor may you transmit it or store it in any other website or other form of electronic retrieval system

Text Copyright © 2020 by Glenn E. Daniels II

Table of Contents

Chapter I 2

Chapter II 5

Chapter III 10

Chapter IV 13

Chapter V 17

Chapter VI 19

Chapter VII 22

Chapter VIII 31

Chapter IX 35

Chapter X 40

Chapter XI 44

Chapter XII 46

Chapter I

It all happened suddenly, the alarm beeping loudly as if to herald soldiers to attack! With a grunt and a groan, Stacey Matthews hit the clock's top with all her might and grunted some more into the pillow. She had just closed her eyes for a moment and now it was 6 am again!

Either way, it had to be done – today was going to be a historic day in the organization, one that she would spearhead, mandated by the Chairman of the Board himself. She was used to these types of things, she was good at her job and after more than ten years of her life put into the organization, there was no one the Chairman of the Board thought better to handle this important task, she was honored and in no way felt nervous about what was to come.

More than anything else, she enjoyed what she did and deemed working with Teaching Technologies as more than a job or something she had to do. She saw it as a calling - her calling. One that was fated to be, and her passion throbbed in tune with her heart in matters regarding the organization.

Teaching Technologies was an organization dedicated to training and growing the next generation of leaders, and to Stacey, there was no greater cause. However, as an N.G.O not moved by profit, but by purpose, there were many challenges the organization faced, and thus, the reason today was very important.

Stacey got up from the bed and heaved a sigh, said some positive words to herself, and began preparations. Teaching Technologies had leadership schools and programs spread across the country, yet in two of those states, the schools seemed to be falling short and not doing as well. If Stacey knew anything, it was that when an organization seemed to be falling, the problem is with its leadership – an issue she was going to address today.

Over the years, she had learned a lot about leadership. It was like yesterday when she started working with Walter Reed, the Chairman of the Board of Teaching Technologies. She was a former student who wanted nothing more than to continue to learn and share with others the breadth of vision and power that Walter taught. She respected him, he was her mentor and she considered herself honored and extremely privileged that he took note of her in their classes, she was a promising student and he seemed impressed by her enthusiasm. Year after year and after a few years of mentorship, Stacey Mathews was recruited into Teaching Technologies as a teacher and a certified leadership coach.

Since then, Stacey had climbed her way up to the top. She was focused, driven and very result oriented. She made mistakes and learned from them and her leadership skills soared every day. At first, she used to work remotely with her staff, giving each one a free hand to carry out tasks, but valuable lessons presented itself at every turn as her staff provided unsatisfactory results and she had to let some people go. But that was all in the past now, she was a better leader who had learned long o that the value of a true leader is how they can **connect with those who follow them as leaders while seeing results and goals achieved as a team.**

Thus, today, she was going to meet with two managers from two different states that had been falling short. With permission from the Chairman of the Board, she had decided to do a retreat with these two managers in form of a series of meetings directed at learning why things were so difficult for them, challenges they faced, and how to achieve better results in their respective state branches. A face to face meeting with them was the best option and she was certain that it would yield fruit.

Just then, the electric kettle whistled, and she poured herself some coffee. She glanced at her clock, it was 8:30 am and the meeting was set for 10 am

Chapter II

The first rule of hosting a meeting was **never to be late and be the first one there.** It was a rule that applied to both online and face to face meetings – a valuable lesson she had learned from her mentor long ago. Hopefully, she would be able to impact these managers and see their fire and result-oriented spirit rekindled and with it, the rise of Teaching Technologies, far above just Texas and the country, but globally as well.

Stacey nosed her way into the driveway and turned off the ignition. It was 10 am sharp. She was thirty minutes early and that was exactly what she wanted. Being the first to be at the meeting room afforded her the time to gather herself and be better prepared for the meeting, also, it set a good example for the managers.

As she got out of the car and headed towards the Teaching Technologies building as if on cue, her phone rang in her bag. She fished for it and smiled when she saw the name across the screen – Walter Reed.

"Hello sir" She said after tapping the answer button and pressing the phone to her ears.

Walter's voice sounded crisp, yet warm on the other end of the line "I remember the meeting retreat is starting today, as scheduled, no hitch?"

"Yes sir. I am heading inside now. Everything is on schedule "Good. Good" Walter said. He was like a father to Stacey and he loved her like the daughter he never had. "Make me proud, Stacey...as always"

Stacey smiled. To be the recipient of such a level of trust was truly flattering and she had a stronger resolve to make these series of meetings as productive as ever. She was armed with all the right strategies for mentoring the managers on how to hold a good meeting, connect with their team, and boost productivity.

She got to the meeting room, took her seat, and set her files before her, made sure to go over the topics of discussions for the day. They were to have several discussions in meetings to come this week and each, she found would be targeted towards solving low productivity rates in their respective branches. Even though she had her agenda, she was going to make this meeting as productive as possible, so she reminded herself of the key things a good host should keep in mind before a meeting:

1. Determine how often to meet with the team ensuring not to organize too many, but the few you do should be incredibly effective and productive

2. Have a clear determination and understanding of the main purpose of the meeting and what It hopes to accomplish

3. The third one was one of the most challenging. Even though Stacey knew the main goal of the meeting, there was a need to break it down into several topics and agenda for different days and further break each agenda into sub-sections and assign time to them each day during the meeting

4. Allowing the participants of the meeting take over sometimes to increase participation as long as they are qualified to handle hosting a meeting

5. Assign roles to the participants of the meeting. As one leads it, let another take the minutes, or watch the time. A meeting should not be

longer than an hour, but there was no reason to be too rigid about that.

6. Get rid of all distractions – declare a ban on all forms of technology (laptops, mobile phones, tablets, etc.).

Stacey smiled to herself, it was like yesterday when she was being tutored by her mentor and now, a decade later, she takes his place as the CEO and yet still remembers everything she had been taught. Hopefully, she would be able to relay this knowledge to the manager and have them execute them in their various branches.

But that was not all, Stacey also completed a quick review of the 8 most important rules of a meeting:

1. State and be clear about the views of the meeting and ask genuine and direct questions. Sometimes participants of a meeting can have dissenting opinions that may divide the meeting and drag it from its main purpose. When you state the view at hand and ask questions that hit the nail on the head, it draws back your participant's inputs to fall in line with the purpose.

2. Be open and share all relevant information integral to the purpose of the meeting so that the participants can be able to help draw out more effective solutions.

3. Do away with ambiguity and explain what the words mean in the context of the meeting. As the host, you are to make sure everyone is of like mind and is focused on the solutions. Kill confusion and lead the meeting to a more productive end.

4. You and the participants must unveil reasons for ideas or opinions and the intent you have in mind. You must allow open conversation and allow each participant to be heard and understood, then jointly decide if the opinion should be taken, allowed, or simply considered.

5. As weird as it may sound, it is wise to steer the meeting away from opinions and arguments. How to do this is to always ensure to shift the focus of the meeting away from talking too much about possible solutions and Identifying the needs that are to be met. Once that is done, the proper path to take would be clearer.

6. Fight against false claims or stories and opinions by fact-checking and testing assumptions.

7. You as the leader must lead the meeting to a joint decision regarding the next steps to take.

8. Leave no agenda item un-covered.

She sat back and relaxed on her chair, feeling confident about the meeting that was about to happen. She had done this a thousand times and these managers would learn a thing or two. She knew what needed to be done, now once again, it was time to see it come into practice in the meeting – a task easier said than done from her experience, but she was ready. She had done this a thousand times and under the great leadership of her mentor, she knew she was up to the task.

She started to focus her mind on how the managers would behave. They were just two and she had read their files: Kate Wilson and Richard Anderson. They were both really promising staff but lately, the reports and surveys from their organization showed failure, mostly due to management issues.

It was Stacey's idea to have a face to face meeting with Ms. Wilson and Mr. Anderson to see how to resolve the situation. It was her show now, a team meeting was the most effective way to deal with the staff and employees and she was certain it would yield the desired results.

From their files, she could see that the managers in question were qualified and seemed equal to the task, there was but a small fundamental issue that was disrupting progress, and that was what needed to be handled here. At least now, *the purpose of the meeting was clear and well defined.*

While Richard has worked his way up in the organization before being transferred to manage the New York branch, Kate was but a new appointee saddled with the responsibility of managing the Wyoming branch. They both had different backgrounds, but their issues were the same. Stacey was glad to be the one chosen to help.

Chapter III

The time was 10:35 am, the managers had arrived on time, and the meeting was about to commence. She exchanged formal pleasantries with the managers and cleared her throat announcing the start of the meeting.

"Thank you all for coming all this way. It shows that you are open to corrections and you realize there is room for improvement." She paused for effect and watched their reactions; their gazes were fixed on her as they stared blankly. "Once again, my name is Stacey Matthews and I would be the leader of this meeting, for today at least." Both Kate and Richard were wondering why she was being so formal now.

"The main purpose of this meeting is to address the reason for the low productivity and trust rate in your respective branches and discover workable solutions on how the matter can be handled better, leading to the desired results." Their gazes were still fixed on her, but this time, they were nodding slowly and thoughtfully to every word she said. Stacey shifted in her seat and continued.

"Over the course of the next few days, we would be discussing several matters on the agenda, several branches of the problem, and come to a few productive solutions on how to move your branches forward. Any questions before we proceed?"

"Yes, if I may" Kate ventured, leaning forward as he spoke "you mentioned we would have this meeting over the course of the next few days?"

"Yes, that's correct" Stacey said

"Pardon me, but is there a reason we cannot work through it all out at once all in one day?"

Stacey smiled; she expected this type of question to be honest. She knew everyone thought she was crazy for suggesting a meeting retreat – a 7-day meeting talking about the same general point and how to address it but she had her reasons and her mentor of all people understood the power of holding this type of meeting more than anyone else and that was why her unorthodox suggestion was approved by him so quickly.

The truth was that in all her years of training and being a leader and a coach, as far as meetings were concerned, she knew that it was **not wise to hold a meeting for more than an hour.** Even though it was okay to be flexible with time, **she knew that a meeting dragged on and on would not only leave the participants mentally exhausted, also prone to distractions, and distractions, she knew were one of the leading causes of unproductivity in the workplace** and she would have none of it.

She explained these reasons to Kate and Kate nodded in agreement and leaned back in her seat. Stacey smiled. It was important to **be open to participants of the meeting and hold nothing back. Share all the valuable information.**

'Now then" Stacey resumed speaking, "shall we proceed?"

"Yes, please" Kate and Richard chorused at the same time as they listened keenly and intently, with just a little skepticism.

"Now, we all know why we are here. Just in case you are unsure, I would clear doubt so we can have a reasonable discourse" Stacey said glancing from Richard to Kate. She knew they most likely knew why there were here, it was sent out in the invitation for this retreat. Another thing Stacey knew was that **the main purpose of the meeting must be spelled out and emphasized even. There must be no ambiguity whatsoever, so everyone can be on the same**

Chapter III

page and offer rational suggestions and solutions borne of a focused mind.

"Before diving into that," Stacey said "I would have you know that the purpose of this meeting is not for some corporate scolding and you are not here to be condemned in any way. The main reason for this meeting is so we can get to the root of the productivity issues in your branches and create some solutions to address them adequately." The managers nodded in relief and Stacey was pleased. Once again, **she was open about what the meeting was about and making sure they were all on the same page.**

"Now, as earlier mentioned, even though we all know the main reason we are here, the reason for the meetings spanning seven days is so we can discuss various agenda and branches of the overall purpose of why we are here. Again, as I mentioned before, it would be **overwhelming to throw it at you all at once**, so I have **broken the main agenda into smaller agendas for discussion.** We would discuss a different part every day and each discussion would bring us closer to our ultimate goal.

At this point, even though the meeting had just started, Stacey was beginning to feel like she was hoarding the time and talking too much. In meetings such as this one, she hated hearing the sound of her own voice and rather favored **involving the participants of the meeting in sharing their opinions.** She decided that she would disclose the purpose of the meeting for today's discussions and allow the managers to do the lion share of the speaking the rest of the day.

Chapter IV

"So, what is on the agenda today, you ask?" Stacey said with a little humor. She pushed her files to the side and laid her hands lightly on the table, facing the two managers squarely. "I can sit here and tell you what I think the problems are and why your teams are not so motivated, but I'll rather not do that. Today, I want to hear from you two, what do you think the problem is? What are the challenges you face with your teams? Honestly, let's discuss what you all feel the problems are and we will know where to go from there" Stacey concluded, leaning back confidently in her chair as if to say 'the floor is yours'. You each have five minutes to share your concerns.

"Mr. Anderson, over to you" Stacey reiterated after a brief moment of silence.

Richard Anderson, Manager of the Teaching Technologies New York branch shifted in his seat and began to speak "Well, Ms. Stacey, first, I'd like to thank you for this opportunity and for not faulting us and being fair enough to try and understand things from our perspective"

Stacey nodded.

"You see, ever since I moved from the Teaching Technologies Texas head office, down to New York, I am forced to work with new people with a different set of ideas and principles. Down here in Texas, things are done more orderly, when you delegate some work to your team, your team gives you updates every other day even though the deadline isn't reached yet, and by this, you as the manager feel carried along and enjoy the fact that you are abreast of the situation. However, over there in New York, things are done differently, first, the city is very boisterous, and everyone is always in rush hour. It appears that this spirit is

Chapter IV

in all New Yorkers. They do not give updates when you delegate work, and they wait till the final deadline before they give an update of things that came up to ruin the assignment. This happens all the time and I have tried to curb it. But no one seems to be listening, they see me as this foreign boss who does not know how things are done there. I am at my wit's end and I try to the best of my ability to make sure it does not happen, but productivity is slow as a result and this is why we are lagging behind"

Stacey nodded again and drew in her breath to speak but was cut short

"It is like I am leading wild humans who live on the edge and take risks all the time. There is no semblance of orderliness like you have here, no respect for the system, and I feel the team does not respect me as a manager. I mean, I do not mean to complain but how am I supposed to lead a team that does not hold me in high esteem. I try to gain their favor, I talk to them, I extend their deadlines, do little favors for them, nothing seems to work. I miss the times when things were simpler and I worked here in the Texas head office, there was order, there is respect for authority and the manager is always carried along. I do not have that and so I---"

Five minutes passed when Stacey jumped in: 'Hold that thought, Mr. Anderson sorry to interrupt like that, but we must hear from Ms. Wilson as well". She said politely smiling at Kate and urging her to speak.

Right there, Stacey did something remarkable and very essential in hosting a meeting. **Even though you must allow each member to talk and air their views, you must ensure that you keep the time hoarders at bay and not be afraid to stop them when they start to take to much time.**

Richard leaned back in his chair and glanced towards Kate who cleared her throat to speak. Kate is a soft-spoken young woman in her early/mid-thirties probably. She had a gentle face but an aura of authority about her. Kate started speaking and Stacey listened intently.

"Well, I fear my situation is much different, perhaps even more serious than that of Mr. Anderson's."

"This is a safe space, Ms. Wilson, please speak" Stacey said. Stacey felt more comfortable now that the managers were doing the talking and she was doing the listening. **In meetings, especially the first, it is important to not make the meeting about you, but about your team and get them to express themselves and talk while you do the listening.**

Kate felt a lot better after hearing that, she let out a grateful smile and resumed speaking." Though serious, the issue with my team is rather simple, also bearing a slight similarity to Mr. Anderson's." Stacey urged her on.

"There does not seem to be any form of motivation or sense of purpose or drive in my team members. It is almost as if they do not understand the purpose and why our organization was started in the first place. They see it just as a job and perhaps something they should do to get paid, but they do not understand the value behind what Teaching Technologies is about. So, there is no serious drive, the desire to do a great job is gone. They only want to do enough to keep their jobs"

"Exactly! That is the major issue, I share the same sentiments about my team members" Richard cut in again. "they do not seem to understand what we stand for; they do not seem to see the vision behind the organization, and therein lies the problem. If only---"

"If I may, Mr. Anderson. We are pressed for time and I would say a few words before finishing up for today"

Mr. Anderson nodded. In another circumstance, perhaps, Stacey would have felt bad for Mr. Anderson, **but she remembered that one of the rules of the meeting is** that the leader of the meeting or whoever the power of moderation falls to must not be afraid of dragging the meeting back to the topic at hand and politely asking one of the members to give another a chance to speak if they hoard the time.

Chapter V

"Thank you, both. So, I have asked you two to tell me what you think the problem is and what the clog in the wheel is towards your team's progress. And you have both presented issues that are a concern. Issues that need to be addressed. However, we will not be talking solutions right now"

The two managers stared at each other, then back at Stacey

"I do not understand. We are only to talk about the challenges and problems alone?" Kate asked, obviously puzzled. Richard nodded in agreement and they both stared at their CEO with an equal measure of confusion.

"...For today, yes. In our next meeting, we will be discussing how we think we can solve the problems on hand and how these issues you have raised can be addressed"

"But...it has been an hour" Richard said, glancing at his watch and frankly looking slightly relieved that the meeting for today was over.

"Yes, that is correct. I do not intend to hold you for more than an hour. We have made progress today and **one effective meeting is more valuable than three trivial meetings.** And this was an effective meeting"

"How so?" Kate asked, her brows furrowing in confusion.

"To find solutions, the first step is to admit the problem. To find the root cause, and that is what you two have done today. You have highlighted the problems and thus, we have made progress. What I would have you do now is to go spend half the day with your counterpart working together and learning and sharing with them. Then go back to your hotels at lunch time, get some rest and start formulating possible solutions that you have not tried yet. Write them down in as much detail as possible and we will discuss them in our next meeting tomorrow."

The two managers nodded.

"It was a pleasure working with you and I'll see you tomorrow" Stacey said, shaking hands with them as they stepped out.

Chapter VI

She sat back down on her chair and let out a deep breath, day one was over, and she had made a lot of observations. She would have to go home and build on what she has discovered so far to be better prepared for the next meeting.

To an outsider, it may perhaps seem that her methods were unorthodox, but they were not. Unlike other meetings where people try to cram in all the topics for discussion in a 4-5 hour meeting, a one-hour meeting where progress was made was more valuable, and even though the managers think that they hadn't made any form of progress, she thought they had and she would reveal why in due time.

She leaned in her chair and tried to playback the meeting in her head. Tomorrow, she knew what was on the agenda, but from the happenings from the meeting today, she will need to change the written agenda for the next day.

Over the years, Stacey Matthews had tried to relate, connect, and better understand people. To her, it was the bedrock of being a successful leader and she thought that was one of the things these managers lacked.

Their characters were very different and she observed it right from the start, Richard, on one hand, seemed to love the sound of his voice and was the type of person who wanted to be in the spotlight and maintain his position as the top dog at all costs. However, Kate, on the other hand, was more of a gentle soul who liked to do things by the book and detested confrontation (perhaps).

Maybe she was just intuitive, or maybe she was perceptive, but Stacey needed to figure these managers out to be able to better connect with them and reach them, and

Chapter VI

in so doing, set an example of how they should treat the members of their respective teams.

There was but only one test to better understand these managers' characters and it was none other than the **DISC TEST**. By tomorrow, she would explain to the managers what the DISC is and what it means for building a team from the ground up. She would explain why mastery of the DISC was a great tool in progressing as a team. But there was another problem Stacey had to address.

As far as this meeting went. It seemed to pick up when the participants were involved and talking and actively taking part in the meeting. She wanted to delegate the meeting to each of them soon.

She knows more than anyone else that **a good leader must not hoard the running of the meetings, they must also give a chance to the participants to take over the meeting and even have assigned roles to each member and parts to play during the meeting.**

But how was she to teach about the DISC formula without hoarding the meeting herself? How was everyone supposed to participate with her speaking all the time? Stacey was confused for a minute, then suddenly, it dawned on her what she must do.

"Phew! Glad that is over" she said to herself as she went over the observations she made from the meeting.

Now, she had to give her mentor an update about how the meeting went and what she thought of the managers. She decided to call him later in the day, for now, she had some other work to do.

■■

Later that evening, Stacey returned home from work, tired and exhausted, mentally, and physically. This was just day one of the meeting retreat, plus all her regular duties and meetings and it was a tad bit stressful. Not to worry, she thought. It would be worth it in the end. She had a fully fortified plan. To the best of her knowledge, she had the solution to the managers' team problems and challenges. However, she did not want to dump it on them. **A good leader does not impose their will during meetings but gently guides and nudges the participants towards excellence.** There had to be productive discussion aimed at finding solutions, they needed to be the ones to create magic and she was just to guide, as an Orchestra Conductor rather than rule like an Emperor.

Just before dinner, Stacey sent the minutes of the meeting, and the assignment Kate and Richard were given. She also sent them the DISC assessment to take tonight and they would score and discuss them in the morning. **After meetings, minutes of the meeting should be sent to all the participants reminding them of what was discussed, as well as their responsibilities for the next meeting.**

Chapter VII

The very next day, Stacey found herself again sitting in the meeting room with the two managers, refreshed and ready to share what they think are the solutions to their problems. It was obvious they had given it some thought and felt they had cracked the case.

"Good morning everyone. Welcome again to this meeting. I realize that yesterday, we talked about how we would each share what we think are the solutions to the problems you both highlighted yesterday as regards the challenges you face with your respective teams.

The two managers nodded their heads eagerly.

"Splendid. Now, I would beg of you to hold that thought until after today. There is something I wish to tell you"

The two participants said nothing but watched with keen interest as Stacey stood up and pulled down the blinds of the windows, then she pressed a button on the remote on a table and the Television on the other side of the wall came to life.

"I would like to show you a slide presentation I prepared for the purpose of this meeting. Please feel free to take down notes as you like, and do not hesitate to ask me any questions during the course of the teaching"

The managers nodded again "Splendid! Let us begin. You see, as managers of your team and branch, and as leadership coaches yourselves, you deal with the most difficult, yet most important resource in the world. What do you think this resource is?"

Stacey paused and looked curiously at the managers with a smile on her face. In this meeting, there was a lot she had to teach, but she needed the meeting to be as interactive as possible and get them all involved.

Chapter VII

Just then, Kate's phone rang and interrupted the flow of the meeting. Stacey froze where she stood. She could not believe she forgot about one of the most important rules of hosting a meeting – **Get rid of distractions including phones, tablets, and any other thing that may divide attention.** It was the first thing Stacey ought to have declared before the meeting even commenced, but now that she was reminded, she quickly made the request that all phones, gadgets, and other technological distractions be put on silence and placed out of view for every meeting.

Kate and Robert obliged, and Stacey was free to proceed.

"Now, where were we --- ah, Yes. I was asking that as leaders we deal with the most important resource on the planet, can anyone tell me what that resource is?"

The two managers stared at each other, then back at Stacy before shrugging.

"...People!" Stacey declared. **"People are the most important resource known to man and as leaders, we must learn to manage this resource. That is your job as the manager of the team."**

Richard raised his hands politely with a confused look on his face.

"But we have tried, how do we manage these people and build trust and confidence that we have not done already?"

Kate nodded in agreement at the question.

"Brilliant question, Mr. Anderson" Stacey echoed " the answer is one word- perhaps the key to all you seek and the thing we do not consider – **CONNECTION"**

Stacey paused for effect and studied the look on their faces as they tried to process the information they had just been given.

"But I have tried to do that, Ms. Stacey. I have tried to be a friend to them, not too tough on them, but they will not budge."

"And you, Ms. Wilson, is this the way you feel as well?"

"Yes!" Kate said emphatically, worry and frustration etched on her brows.

"Great, the agenda for today is to talk about connecting with them, but the question is how, right? Well, each of you has narrated stories about how you did things to prove yourself as friends to your staff and team members and you've done your best to make them follow and respect you."

The managers were nodding vehemently in agreement.

"...But the connection I speak of now does not even require you to do anything, all you have to do is seek to understand each and every one of your team members, once you do, it would be easier to relate with them. Everyone likes someone else who understands them, so if their manager understands them, they would be more malleable towards purpose and easier to lead toward excellence."

"So how do you propose we understand our team members, Ms. Stacey?" Kate asked in her gentle tone, it was obvious that her interest was piqued, and she wanted to learn a lot more, but did not want to "rock the boat".

"Simple, Mrs. Wilson, apply the DISC formula. The DISC formula is a chart that highlights and categorizes the four types of people on your team. Highlighting their likes, dislikes, what they want, their strengths, and their weaknesses. In the long run, you would better be able to deal with them, respond to them, and relate with them accordingly.

The DISC represents the four quadrants of people and behaviors and we shall be dealing with and examining them one after the other. Let us start with quadrant "D", shall we?

Stacey pushed a button on the TV remote and the first slide show she had prepared, appeared on the screen as the managers stared on with keen interest. The first slide looked something like this:

THE DISC QUADRANT
"D"

Characteristics
- *Confidence*
- *Boldness*
- *Self-centeredness, asking "What's in it for me?"*
- *Being domineering*
- *Strengths*
- *Being great problem solvers*
- *Having the ability to make quick decisions*
- *Being goal-oriented and following through on goals*
- *Being great team leaders*
- *Weaknesses*
- *High D's lack caution.*
- *They have a tendency to overrun people.*
- *Because of this, people will sometimes try to steer clear of the D.*
- *When a high D rolls over you, call them out by politely saying "Whoa, you're*
- *Steamrolling over the top of me."*
- *High D's are impulsive and often need people to slow them down.*
- *Fears*
- *They fear being taken advantage of.*

- *They fear losing control.*

Stacey paused to watch the manager's reactions. Then she went on to explain each and every segment of the D quadrant, how these are the people that appear confident, bold, and always want to be in the spotlight. They love to lead, and they love to take credit for good deeds, they also come off as domineering. However, they can be amazing team leaders, they usually have the ability to think on the spot, they are goal-oriented and actually ambitious if you push them enough, generally, they are amazing problem solvers.

"So, take a minute now and think back to every one of your team members." Stacy asked. "Take a few minutes to discuss each person in your office that would fit into the "D" category and share with each other how best to connect with them. Create your answer together and share it with me in five minutes. The clock is running."

The two managers worked for five minutes than asked for more time. Stacey gave them five more minutes.

Stacey was right, they did recognize these attributes in some of their team members. However, Stacey realized that Richard was a bit uneasy as they worked.

She knew why he was so uneasy - he had just realized he was among those in the D quadrant as well and he did not care for it. Good for him, Stacey thought, at least now he would know how to deal with others like him.

Stacey had Kate and Richard explain the strengths and weaknesses of those in the D quadrant. Stacey added one more point for emphasis. "Make sure you play to their strengths rather than their weaknesses. The strength of the "D" will drive your team to success."

"Any questions?" she asked as she concluded on the quadrant and moved to hit the button for the next slide.

"None, please proceed" Kate said. Stacey could see that she was learning a lot and that made her feel great. Richard still said nothing. Stacey turned toward him and said "D" are not bad people.

"Now, we move on to the 'I' quadrant. The slide of the quadrant in question appeared on the screen:

"I"

Characteristics
As leaders, they are:
- *Inspirational*
- *Laid-back*
- *Hard working*
- *In general, they are:*
- *Optimistic*
- *Fun-loving*
- *Persuasive*
- *Impulsive*
- *Strengths*
- *Great motivators*
- *Entertaining and funny*
- *Strong communicators*
- *Great collaborators*
- *Weaknesses and fears*
- *High I's are too trusting.*
- *They are overly concerned about others.*
- *They have time management issues and often run late.*
- *They fear loss of friendships.*

Like the first time, Stacey gave a little pause for effect and allowed the managers to go through the slide. They read with keen interest and this time; it was Kate that seemed uneasy. She was an "I".

Stacey asked that they do the same process for 'I's" as they did for "D's" giving them ten minutes.

Once again both Kate and Richard started to see the attributes of the "I" personality type and was able to create a plan to connect better with them.

Stacey explained that 'I's may have their weaknesses but can be very valuable on the team if you recognize it. When you connect with team members based on who they are rather than who you want them to be, you have an amazing combination of trust, motivation, and productivity.

Stacey stopped taking and paused again. She took a sip of water and asked if there were any questions before they closed.

"None, Ms. Stacey" but I would like to discuss some more things about some of my team members to better understand how to deal with them".

Stacey paused. The time was fast spent and she didn't want to spend more than an hour for their meeting so they do not get mentally exhausted and lose productivity or worse, get distracted, but she remembered another of the rules of meetings.

Even though you should ensure not to go beyond one hour, do not be rigid. Allow constructive and productive discussions. This being said, what Kate wanted to point out seemed to be productive and so Stacey decided not to be rigid and allow it.

"Sure, Mrs. Wilson, let us hear your thoughts" Stacey said, sitting down and taking another sip of water.

"Thank you. So, while I realized that the two quadrants are very different. In my mind, when I go over some of the members of the team, I find that some of them have exhibited characteristics that draw from the two quadrants. It is hard to pinpoint which one they are in and so it would

Chapter VII

be harder to relate with them because I will still not understand them"

"Hmm. You pose an important question" Stacey realized that Richard had not spoken for a while. She decided to draw him in, **in meetings, the leader must always ensure to involve everyone and make no one feel left out in participation.**

"Mr. Anderson. What do you think? Is such a thing possible? For one member of the team to exhibit characteristics that belong to more than one of the quadrants. What are your thoughts on this?

Richard leaned forward and stared into thin air. He appeared to be thinking, Stacey knew to **allow the silence to become a powerful partner,** so she just let it happen. After a few seconds, he cleared his throat and began to speak.

"Well. I would suppose it is possible. Human beings can be very unpredictable. But I must confess, I would not know what to do in such an instance or how to relate with the team member." How do I know what motivates them and what is important to them?

"Well said, Mr. Anderson. I think you are right. It may be possible for a single human to exhibit more than one of the quadrants, but as the manager, you are to know your team members in and out. Study them and aim to understand them, you would realize they are more dominant in one of the quadrants than the other.

Kate nodded aggressively as her mind was once again cast upon her team members. And without warning, and out of character, Kate said loudly. "I will ask each person on my team what is most important to them when it comes to this job."

Stacey was shocked at the force that Kate had said this, and Richard was equally shocked.

"There, does that answer your question?" Stacey said to them both.

"Accurately and completely. Thank you" Kate responded.

"So, shall we call it a day now and regroup tomorrow to finish the other two quadrants?"'

"Yes, please" Kate and Richard echoed.

They talked for a few more minutes and the two managers left the room. Kate was exhausted and left with a headache.

The next day, someone else must take control of the meeting. Stacey could not help but feel she was leading by example. While Stacey **knew the right thing to do was to assign roles to the members during the meeting.** Stacey would continue that practice for the next meeting.

After a while, Stacey got up from her chair and left the room. That night, **she sent out minutes of the meeting for the last time and assigned roles to each member. The email stated that Richard was to lead the next meeting while Kate would take the minutes.** And with that, Stacey felt relieved.

She took up her phone and called her mentor to give him a breakdown of how the meetings were going and she went straight to bed with high hopes for how tomorrow would turn out.

Chapter VIII

The next day, everyone assembled in the meeting room again, and like before Stacey read the minutes of the meeting and handed over the meeting to Richard who seemed to enjoy the spotlight. (of course)

She handed him the TV remote for the slideshows and requested that he explain what he thought the other two quadrants were all about, taking a cue from the last meetings they had.

He pushed a button on the remote and the next slide show came up:

"S"
Characteristics
- Loyal
- Steady
- Restful
- Calming
- Patient
- Strengths
- They concentrate on the task at hand.
- They are not easily interrupted.
- They typically specialize in one thing.
- They have fortitude and will not quit or give up.
- They have the ability to stay calm and do not get easily frustrated.

Weaknesses
- High S's are very possessive.
- They can be too hospitable.

- They are very slow to change and require lots of advanced notice for impending change.

Kate focused on the screen and seemed to be deep in thought as she nodded slowly. She realized that she may have had some little qualities of an "I", but she was predominantly an "S".

As Richard began to explain, Kate took down the minutes while Stacey supervised and watched the time. **A meeting where all the members participate is a perfect meeting.**

At the end of the explanation and exercise, Stacey reiterated how the strengths are what should be played upon and used as an advantage.

As the leader, Richard asked if there were any more questions. There were none, so he went on to the last slide:

"C"

Characteristics
- Accurate
- Tactful
- Systematic
- Strengths
- They love details.
- They are very careful.
- They are into preventative maintenance.
- They have very high standards and are very demanding of themselves.
- Weaknesses and fears
- High C's can be overly precise.
- They have a tendency to procrastinate.
- They will stall due to their lack of decision-making ability.
- They can be lousy delegators.
- They fear criticism of their work.

Chapter VIII

Richard plunged into the explanation and exercise for the last quadrant just like he learned from Stacey. Reiterated that the strength of the quadrant is what will help the organization if it is utilized properly. He went on and on and held on to the spotlight he was enjoying with pontification and repetition.

Stacey looked at her watch and realized Richard had taken more time than expected.

Stacey announced "Great, That's amazing, Mr. Anderson. We are at our time limit for this section."

Once again. Stacey had demonstrated what a good timekeeper should do – **not be afraid to call out someone who is taking all the time**.

Richard surprised everyone by saying "Thank you Ms. Stacey for keeping us on track."

The meeting came to an end after some more discussions about the quadrants and Stacey decided to help round it off.

"So now, do you still stand by the potential solutions you were asked to provide two days ago?" she asked the managers.

They both smiled and shook their heads no. In light of new revelations, they realized that there was more to the behavior of their team members and they had been going about it all wrong.

Exactly the fact Stacey Matthews wanted to nudge them towards. **Not to tell them but have them discover it.**

"Now, any more questions before we wrap up for today?"

They both shook their heads.

"Splendid! Mr. Anderson. Good job today, and Kate, well done on taking the minutes of the meeting. We will be expecting it in our emails by the end of today. Have a nice day everyone. Please spend most of the day with people here in the home office that can be of help to you when you return to your office." Stacey added, "Please prepare a written report on what you are learning from your counterparts here and...and what personality type they are.

The meeting ended, and everyone left the room, leaving Stacy pleased and happy. She did not feel as exhausted and she was glad everyone else had the chance to participate in one way or the other. It was a great and productive meeting.

Yet a bigger challenge surprise was yet to come.

Chapter IX

That night, the Chairman of the Board, Walter Reed called Stacey to ask how the meetings were going and if they were making any progress. Stacey gave a full report and as usual, Walter was proud of her. After the call, Stacey ran over to her laptop and sent the managers an emergency email.

There was to be no meeting tomorrow morning – physically, at least. The Chairman of the Board wanted to have an online conference meeting with all of them and so there was no need to meet in the morning.

The meeting is scheduled for 2 pm the next afternoon and Kate and Richard were to host it. Stacey could not help but wonder why Walter wanted to see the participants now before the meetings were even over, but he knew best, and she looked forward to tomorrow's meeting. It would be fun to watch how Kate and Richard would run the meeting. Stacey delegate it all to them after she would give them the agenda (as much as she knew) and have them blaze forward with it.

The next day, at 12:30 pm, Stacey, Kate, and Richard took their seats in the office with laptops ready in front of them. Stacey reviewed all the rules of hosting a great online meeting:

1. *Set an Agenda*
2. *Do some practice*
3. *Stay focused*
4. *As the host, be the first on the call*
5. *Make sure to introduce everyone*
6. *Keep up the pace*
7. *Create a flow*
8. *Do some recap in the end*

Chapter IX

  9. Follow up.

Then she left the room and let them prepare together. It was now 1:45 pm and Stacey logged into the meeting. Another rule: **as an online host, be the first person on the call.**

She waited for a few moments and eventually, the managers appeared on the meeting video connection as well as Mr. Walter Reed himself. Everyone was in a different room by design.

"Good afternoon everyone" Kate began. "You are all welcome to today's virtual meeting. Great to see you, Mr. Reed"

He nodded and smile back.

As per the agenda Stacey was to handle the introduction.

"Mr. Anderson, Ms. Wilson, allow me to introduce the visionary, founder and head leader of Teaching Technologies, Mr. Walter Reed. And Mr. Reed...these are the managers from the New York branch and the Wyoming branch offices, – Mr. Richard Anderson and Ms. Kate Wilson, respectively.

She gave them some time to exchange pleasantries. Stacey had just stuck by one of the most important rules of online meetings. **Make Introductions when necessary.** It should be the first thing you do to get the participants more acquainted with one another.

After the pleasantries, Kate took over the meeting to **keep the flow.**

"Mr. Reed asked that to meet with all of us today. I am sure he has a very important purpose and some nuggets of wisdom to drop for us today. I will be handing over the meeting to him to hear what he has to say"

"Mr. Reed, Over to you"

"Well, thank you, Ms. Kate. I truly commend your efforts. Well, I would not take much of your time, but the purpose of this meeting is to hear from the managers how they are getting along and to know what both think about the meetings so far."

Stacey smiled. She now understood why Mr. Reed wanted this meeting. It was a feedback meeting.

Getting the feedback was one of the most important things when you are working with a team and Mr. Reed wanted to point that out.

"So, I would start with you, Mr. Anderson."

"Yes sir." Richard confirmed on his end of the line.

"Good. So please, from your personal experiences so far, what do you think of the meetings you have had so far with Ms. Stacey and your colleague? Have you learned something valuable so far and would you say this meeting is helping you as a manager"

Mr. Anderson smiled on his end of the connection and began to speak

"Yes, Mr. Reed. I must confess that at first, I didn't have high hopes because I wasn't sure if a meeting retreat would solve the issues we have, but Ms. Stacey has been incredibly amazing and my eyes have been gradually opening to the things that I never considered may be the cause of the productivity and inefficiency amongst my team members. Me. Initially, I thought I had it all figured out and I felt the solution was transferring me from there to somewhere else. I felt that my team in New York were difficult to work with and their work ethic was responsible for the slow progress we are making, now...with the help, guidance, and mentoring of Ms. Stacey, I have realized how foolish that was and it is becoming clearer the next step to take. The meetings have been productive and insightful"

Richard finished and nodded in gratitude.

Chapter IX

"That warms my heart to hear, Mr. Anderson. Mrs. Mathews is one of our best and brightest, a true visionary in herself and you would do well to pick her brains and learn from her. It would help solve the issues you have on the ground."

Mr. Reed smiled again and turned to Kate on his screen.

"How about you, Kate? Tell me your thoughts on the teachings and meeting so far?"

"Well, sir. I have really learned and enjoyed every bit of the meetings thus far. I was initially confused about the next steps to take, but during the course of these meetings, as my colleague stated, It had been becoming clearer on what needs to be done and the meetings so far have been productive. I cannot wait to see what is next on Ms. Stacey's agenda for us"

Mr. Reed cracked a proud smile and gave a small clap.

"Well, Done, Ms. Wilson. I expected nothing less. Now, over to you"

"Thank you, sir, and thank you all. It has really been an honor meeting with you all these past few days and interacting, we still have a couple of meetings left and I am glad you are already getting so much from the meeting. Mr. Reed, anything else you would like to add?"'

"Yes" Mr. Reed said from the other line "I wish you all the best of luck and I hope you both become the landmark leaders I know you are. But I have one more question. Can you take this back to your teams and teach them?" Part of your assignment this evening will be to create a plan to teach all that you will learn with Ms. Stacey to your lead managers when you return. Thank you both."

Everyone echoed their thanks and Kate brought the meeting to a close.

They had fulfilled all the duties of a true leader hosting an online meeting and Stacey was proud of Kate and

Richard. There are a few more meetings left for them after which they would all reach a conclusion on how to progress in their respective locations. For now, she was glad that the feedback was great, and she knew that the managers themselves had learned the importance of getting feedback as the manager. She knew they would take that lesson with them when they returned to their teams, and she was happy that she was imparting these managers through simple one-hour meetings. **There is nothing that cannot be achieved after a productive and effective meeting.**

Chapter X

The next day, Stacey was back in the meeting room with both managers and she immediately welcomed them and commenced the meeting.

"Now, before we go to today's agenda, allow me to speak briefly on feedback and the importance of receiving feedback. With your various teams, asides from connecting and understanding them, you should also aim to receive honest feedback from your teams during your meetings. If you decide something or you want to be sure the meeting is going or went as you planned, consider asking them for honest feedback and it'll help you know you are on the right track. You are a leader, not a boss, and as such, you owe some form of responsibility to your team to ensure they are comfortable with how you choose to lead them"

She turned to Richard

"Mr. Anderson. It was on this very table you sat three days ago and complained about how your team in New York does not seem to favor updating you on projects and deadlines. It seemed to upset you and you were convinced that was one of the causes of inefficiency and unproductivity in your branch. Well, since you realize how important it is for your team to give feedback, you have shown that it is important for you to give feedback to your team as well, it is that simple"

Richard nodded his agreement and seemed to be processing a lot. Kate was also fixed on Stacey and was obviously processing a lot.

"Any questions so far?" Stacey asked

There was none, so she moved on

"Lady and gentleman. I realize that we have four days left after today for our meetings, but tomorrow, no meeting shall be held. **There is no point in having a meeting just because it was scheduled.** I can see that we are all making good progress, so there is no need to overstretch this. On the final day of this topic, we will talk about the solutions together and practical ways on how to motivate and build trust with our team members.

"Today, I would just like to go over with you all the nuggets and tactics I have used with you both throughout these meetings we have held. Spend the rest of the day working with the staff here and making notes on things you can improve. Please prepare a written report for me concerning who has helped you and any feedback that you may have.

"Let me share a few tools I've used to build trust and confidence between us and practice it within your team during team meetings"

"So, from the moment you walked in here and we made acquaintance...the first thing I did was to spell out what exactly the purpose of the meeting was. I know you both had ideas already, but it is important when you are meeting with your respective teams to spell out the purpose of the meeting'"

"The second thing I did was to break down the purpose and agenda of the meetings into smaller bits, so we do not get overwhelmed. Even though the purpose of our meeting was to increase productivity within your team, we did not thrash it all out in one day, we had meetings different days after that and each day had a different sub-agenda. When you meet with your teams, imbibe this and you would have really effective meetings"

"Thirdly, you all may have realized that even though I hosted the first meeting, I ensured that in the later

meetings, you both had a role to play. So, in the second meeting, while Richard was hosting, I had Kate take the minutes of the meeting and send it out to us all, after, while I watched the time. When you are meeting with your teams, allocate responsibilities. You may have more than two people on your team and that is even better. Let them participate in the meeting somehow"

"You would also see that I was open to involving you both in the meetings we had. Apart from delegating responsibilities in the meetings, I also made sure your opinions and voices were heard. One when a person speaks, I would call on the other, just to make sure you participate. Do this with your team as well, during meetings. Let everyone be involved.

"Furthermore, you may have realized that I always tried for each meeting not to be longer than an hour, but I was not rigid with the time. One time, Mrs. Wilson had to talk about something constructive even after the time had elapsed, but I allowed it, why? Because as a rule a meeting should not go beyond an hour, you should still be open for productive and constructive discussions even if it goes longer."

"Now, you would also see that from the beginning of this meeting, I never imposed anything or solutions on you both. I allowed us to rub minds and asked direct questions"

"Lastly, Mr. Anderson" Stacey said, while smiling "you would find that on more than one occasion, I had to stop you to give Kate a chance to speak. As the leader of the meeting, you must ensure that everyone speaks and that means stopping whoever is overdoing it even though they may be making great points like yourself or just full of passion. Remember someone making great points like you *were doing, it is hard to stop them because you want to hear them."*

Richard smiled "Understood"

Stacey went on to state a few other things she had done to build trust and communication, thus creating productivity and trust in their meetings and the managers learned a great deal.

"Great!" Stacey said when they were finished. "get some rest tomorrow, do some thinking, and we will have our next meeting on Friday and discuss the next step to take based on what we have talked about. Richard you will run that meeting. Work with Kate to establish the agenda. It is all yours, yes Sir all yours.

The managers thanked her and left, and Stacey was happy the meetings was finally coming to an end. Not because she was exhausted, which she was, but because she was glad her plan worked, and the meetings were productive and effective already.

Chapter XI

On Friday Kate and Richard was surprised to see all the Senior Managers in the room. Stacey told them to use this meeting to practice what they learned as it was to serve as a review to everyone else and some great feedback for both.

"Ladies and Gentlemen. "Richard started." The purpose of this meeting is to fully discuss the solutions, agree on the next steps to take to boost productivity amongst our teams back home based on what we have learned so far. I want to urge everyone to be respectful of each other's opinions and not go off track.

The managers shifted in their seats and nodded, and the meeting began!

In the meeting, both managers had different opinions that were of the same goal. While Richard wanted to have one on one meetings with his team members to get to know them, Kate was of the opinion that having a general meeting with all of them to get to know and understand them better works best.

The entire room argued about the matter for few minutes before Stacey put an end to it. She saw this coming and she was prepared, she began to speak.

"So, here is what we should consider doing. Richard, I need for you to argue Kates point and convince the rest of the room and Kate you are going to argue Richards point and convince the room as well. You will find that this is a short cut if you can get people to truly argue the other persons point of view. Let's try it.

"Ok, good. Now which of your models best fits this need?"

Chapter XI

Both managers agreed the need is to build connection and trust and depending on the personality of your team you will sometimes use one-on-one or team meetings.

There was a pause, but they had to agree one on one meetings was a better option to get to know people on your team. Stacey was proud.

If discussing solutions is becoming chaotic, shift the focus and discuss about NEEDS, the solution would appear.

In the end, they agreed on the next steps to boost productivity.

Chapter XII

MAIN IDEA: Build trust and productivity amongst team members.

HOW:
- *Do one on one meetings and speak individually with each team member.*
- *Have FEEDBACK DAYS once every month where the members give feedback on how they have run things and in turn the managers would receive feedback on how they have been so far.*
- *Use the DISC formula to play to member's strengths and not on the weakness*
- *Share the goals of TEACHING TECHNOLOGIES in the members of the teams every day.*

In less than 6 months, the branches in Wyoming and New York reported significant improvements in their productivity and it was all because of effective meetings.

www.ingramcontent.com/pod-product-compliance
Lightning Source LLC
Chambersburg PA
CBHW031553210526
45464CB00003B/1284